Love Jen

LOVE
Courtship
&
Marriage

*being an Invaluable and
Instructive Guide
for the
Romantically Inclined*

HUGH EVELYN LONDON

This edition first published in 1967
by Hugh Evelyn Limited
9 Fitzroy Square, London W1P 5AH
and © 1967, Hugh Evelyn Limited

Reprinted 1970, 1971

Designed by Lawrence Edwards

Printed in Great Britain by
Burgess & Son (Abingdon) Ltd.

SBN 238 78880 6

Contents

LOVE, COURTSHIP AND MARRIAGE

To be married is to be happy. In contracting marriage many blunder through ignorance into a lifetime of weal or woe To help remove this lack of knowledge we have prepared the following pages.

The sciences of Phrenology, Physiology and Physiognomy throw so much light, and have such an important bearing upon love, courtship and marriage, as to render their teachings of the highest importance in these matters. Phrenology illustrates the faculties of the mind; it shows that the domestic propensities fill a large space in the base and back of the brain, and have an important influence on character. Moral and intellectual faculties should control social feelings and as a means to this end we recommend young men to engage in physical exercises, and both sexes to join in social recreations, mingling in virtuous society, and avoiding the reading of coarse and corrupting books. The virility of manhood should not be wasted in youth, but last to a good old age. It is this waste of vitality by the abuse of the love principle that fills the world with imbeciles, misanthropes, invalids and suicides.

THE SOCIAL FACULTIES

The social faculties are located at the lower and back part of the head, causing it to project behind the ears. Their size and activity create most of the family affections and aspirations. The principal organ of the social group is:

1. AMATIVENESS

Fig. 1.	Fig. 2.
Amativeness Large. Aaron Burr, noted for his debauchery.	Amativeness Moderate.

Its location is at the back of the head, when prominent imparting a fullness behind and between the ears. Its function is to draw the sexes together with the magnetic power of love. Those who lack this organ or abuse it become morose, unsocial, and deficient in prudence and firmness. In olden times those men who had this faculty large were said to be courteous, gallant, chivalrous protectors and admirers of womankind.

Fig. 3.	Fig. 4.
Amativeness Very Small.	Amativeness Perverted, indicating Sensuality.

Men who possess large Amativeness, combined with development of Friendship and strong Vitality, enjoy the company of the female sex intensely; while those who have small Amativeness rather avoid the society of women, and sometimes evince a want of refinement, respect and delicacy of feeling in their intercourse with them. Small Amativeness is content with platonic attachment rather than passionate love.

Happy marriage is promoted when both husband and wife possess a full development of Amativeness. When the organ is very large in one partner and small in the other, there cannot be much connubial bliss. When this faculty and constitution are both feeble amatory indulgence is certain to cause debility, and probably early death. Husbands who truly love their wives should in such cases exercise self-control, and as a means to this end, engage in active bodily exercise, practise temperance in eating and drinking and, if necessary, occupy a separate bed or bedroom.

2. PHILOPROGENITIVENESS
or the Love of Children

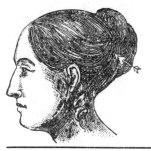

Fig. 5.
Philoprogenitiveness
Large.

Fig. 6.
Philoprogenitiveness
Small.

This faculty is situated in the middle of the back head and is naturally more developed in women than in men. This organ is the fountain of motherly love. Remove it and the new-born infant would be tended only from a sense of duty and not with love. When the faculty is in excess or uncontrolled it leads fond mothers to 'spoil' their little ones by indulgence and want of firmness. Alas for the poor children in school or at home when teachers and mothers are deficient in the faculty. It is more pleasing to dwell upon full possession of Philoprogenitiveness as in the following lines:

'O God!', she cried, in accents wild,
'If I must perish, save my child!'
She stripped the mantle from her breast,
And bared her bosom to the storm,
And round the child she wrapped the vest,
And smiled to think her child was warm.
With one cold kiss, one tear she shed,
And sank upon her snowy bed.

A greater proportion of English mothers suckle their children than in France or in the United States, and this is one reason why the people of England are noted for their robustness, comeliness, and longevity. It is this faculty that causes girls to love their dolls, boys their pet birds and rabbits, spinsters their parrots and men their dogs and horses.

3. ADHESIVENESS OR FRIENDSHIP

This faculty has an important influence upon man's relationships. Without it he would be as solitary as

Robinson Crusoe. Adhesiveness imparts warmth of feeling, impulse, energy in greeting friends with smiles, cordial handshaking and sometimes hugging, kissing, slapping and other tokens of personal attachment. People who have Adhesiveness largely developed visit and write to their friends often. It is a characteristic of the Hebrew people to the present day. It is also strong in the people of Scotland and Ireland.

| Fig. 7. | Fig. 8. |
| Adhesiveness Large. | Adhesiveness Small. |

4. INHABITIVENESS

Essentially an English or Anglo-Saxon faculty constituting a strong love of home. Our kindred over the seas often call Old England their 'home', and the Scots, Welsh and Irish whilst prone to roam remain passionately attached to their native lands.

| Fig. 9. | Fig. 10. |
| Conjugality Large. | Conjugality Small. |

This is a truly domestic quality and forms the foundation of marriage. In combination with Amativeness it generates the desire to be become united with one of the opposite sex for life. Married life is not only the happiest but the healthiest. The tables of Insurance and Benefit Societies show that married people live longer than the unmarried. Marriage is also favourable to a virtuous life. The criminal class is largely composed of unmarried persons.

CONDITIONS ESSENTIAL
TO HAPPY WEDLOCK

Young persons are apt to dress up the institution of marriage in their imagination with so many garlands of pleasure that it appears to be a state of ethereal joys, unclouded skies and paradisiacal blessedness; but it must be remembered that the joys of marriage grow out of duty and truthfulness.

When a young woman gets married and thinks that she may then take life easily and do little or nothing for the comfort of her husband then she is sure to be disappointed. The same applies to the husband. If either fail in their duties, wedlock will soon be shorn of its expected enjoyments.

Before people enter into marriage let them be as sure as Phrenological science can make them that they are suited to the nature and requirements of each other. Phrenology explains differences of taste, temper and disposition and would never sanction a match between incongruous natures. Some of these differences will be shown later in this book. Meanwhile let us first take a look at the bachelor.

THE BACHELOR

Marriage is the natural state of man but some men are afraid to marry because they think they cannot afford to keep a wife. We should advise the ladies not to fret after men of this kind inasmuch as they possess too little spirit. Let us take a glance at the life of an old bachelor.

He may have been a respectable commercial traveller who starts out in the morning after partaking of his unsocial breakfast. While transacting his day's business he meets with worry and anxiety. Perhaps he may have got wet and longs to get home to change his clothes. When he reaches his lodgings, earlier than usual, he finds the home locked up, the landlady having gone out. He waits for her return, and on entering everything is cold and cheerless and the fire is out. Should he complain the landlady quickly informs him that she will not stay in all day merely to please him and if he is not satisfied he can find other lodgings. His wet clothes make him chilly, but the clean linen is also damp and may eventually cause a fever. He is then laid upon a bed of affliction and his landlady will complain of this inconvenience, while the bachelor, pain racking his brow, will be acutely conscious that he has no loving wife to smooth his pillow and administer to his comfort. Perhaps his life may be cut short in consequence of careless nursing. Should he rally he returns to work feeling a sad longing for something, he knows not what.

There is a wonderful contrast between the life of this bachelor and that of the happily married man . . . whose wife anxiously thinks of him. She remains at home, keeps a good fire in the grate, sees that his linen is well aired, the buttons all on, and his slippers ready for his use. When she hears his footsteps, the tea and toast are already prepared, and everthing is bright and comfortable. After tea she drives away his cares by singing him one of her cheerful songs.

WHY MEN AND WOMEN
DESIRE TO MARRY

The observer of human nature must have noticed the various reasons which induce men to marry, from the lowest—the love of money or sensuality, to the highest—the love of purity, truth, fidelity, and all those virtuous feelings that emanate from a congenial union between one man and one woman.

One man marries for a home. He is tired of his bachelor life, its solitariness and sameness, and wants a change. He has pictured to himself the delights of home life, the cosy fireside, pleasant chats with his wife, and romps with his children. He knows nothing of the discomforts of married life and expects to be as happy as the day is long, Let us hope that he will never be deceived.

A young woman may wish to marry because she is tired of working hard at dress-making, teaching or some other ill-paid employment, and wants a home of her own. She also thinks that marriage is one long honeymoon.

Other young women marry because they dread being called 'old maids', or because they think it must sound so respectable to be called Mrs So-and-So, or because they want sympathy, and even out of spite! The majority, we hope, marry for love, which is the very best reason why men and women should desire to marry.

MARRYING FOR MONEY is usually a despicable motive, though there may be extenuating circumstances which seem to justify such a course in certain cases, such as business necessities or the care of a young family. Wealth is a good thing in itself, and when rightly used may be a source of happiness to its possessor and a benefit to the world: but to make it the leading motive for matrimony is to turn it into a snare and a curse, and cupidity will be found to be a greater tormentor than Cupid.

As a rule, people should marry in their own rank of life, as near as possible. If a young lady who has been brought up in the lap of luxury and never taught to do anything were to marry an unpecunious man who could not afford to keep a servant, her life would be one of complete drudgery; and if she had been accustomed to entertain company and go into society, the deprivation of these enjoyments would be mortifying in the extreme. It may be romantic to read in a sensational novel of a lord marrying a milkmaid, but such unequal matches do not answer well in real life.

Some persons marry for beauty. It is said that 'a thing of beauty is a joy for ever.' This is true, but if a man marries a woman for her beauty and nothing more it is evident that his love will vanish when wrinkles take possession of her brow, when elasticity leaves her step, and when her lips become livid and white.

WHOM NOT TO MARRY

When you see a young woman with her shawl fastened all awry and fractures in her clothes, they are pretty sure signs that she reads novels and lies in bed late of a morning; and if she has holes in her stockings, an unwashed face and a slovenly appearance, do not be misled by her bright eyes and cherry lips. A girl who cannot find time to keep herself tidy, clean and prim, ought not to be trusted with the care of shirt buttons, stocking mending, and ironing, to say nothing about the husband for whom these articles are required.

When a young lady entertains you with spicy

ridicule of her gentlemen friends, 'showing up' their various imperfections and weaknesses, take up your hat and go. If you were to marry such a person you would be sure to have a full share of her ridicule and unkind criticism.

When a young lady cares more about novels and romances than she does about history or other useful knowledge it is a sign that there are rooms 'to let' in the 'upper stories.' Avoid marrying a lady who cannot do anything that requires a little extra exertion, unless you have plenty of money to keep a servant.

Place no confidence whatever in the 'flirt', or any young lady who boasts of her many 'conquests.' Such persons usually have more susceptibility of mind than strength of love, and they are as likely to jilt you as their former lovers. Avoid marrying a woman who has had several disappointments in love, because such disappointments have a tendency to render her suspicious of everybody; moreover it is not in the power of human nature for the heart to be given wholly to one person when it has been previously devoted to others.

OBJECTIONABLE QUALITIES IN A WIFE

A man should not marry a woman of an hysterical temperament. Tears may be tolerated in the honeymoon, but afterwards they become a bore. The man is to be pitied who is wedded to a woman who, on the least provocation, throws herself into a fit of hysterics.

One of the most unpleasant sights to a physiologist is to see women walking about with wasp-like waists. Avoid such women as you would the plagues of Egypt. They must be vain and foolish to torture themselves into such an ugly and unnatural shape; and it is impossible for them to give birth to healthy children. Better to have no wife at all than one with a very small waist.

It is not prudent for large men to marry little women; yet we often see that big men marry little women, and big women little men. There are physiological reasons why such matches are unsuitable.

Do not be entrapped by a merely pretty face, and keep not company with a young woman who is extravagantly fond of ornament. The best adornment of the other sex is a meek and quiet spirit; and the most suitable ornament in the shape of precious metal is the circlet of gold, which is the emblem of union with a kindred spirit. The common use of false shapes and forms by women is very much to be deprecated, being both deceptive and unhealthy.

Avoid marrying a woman who is constitutionally lazy and indolent. No matter how hard her husband may work, or how great his income may be, he will find his strength, patience and money all too little to support a helpless being. An indolent woman is almost sure to be fretful and peevish, because she has nothing to do but brood over her real troubles and create imaginary ones. An indolent and extravagant woman will always keep her husband poor; hence the old proverb, 'A man must ask his wife whether he may live.'

OBJECTIONABLE QUALITIES
IN A HUSBAND

Ladies would do well to avoid the 'nice young man' who is paying them particular attention but who speaks sharply to his mother and omits to pay his sisters those little attentions and courtesies that come so gracefully from men to women; for these are signs that, as a wife, he will expect you to put up with the same neglect as soon as the first blossoming of the wedding season is over. It is well also to be cautious how you place your faith in gentlemen who wear diamond scarf pins and spend their leisure time on hotel steps, in playing billiards, in gambling or in leading a fast life, for it is probable they belong to that extensive class of society for whom Satan is usually supposed to find some mischief still for them to do. It is much better to lavish your smiles on a sturdy young farmer, carpenter, or even labourer, who work by the day in their shirt sleeves. Ladies would also do well to avoid the 'masher' and the young man who thinks so much better of himself as to believe that the young ladies are not good enough for him.

Do not marry a bad man in the hope of 'reforming' him. Many badly organised men have made fair promises, vowing that they would reform if the object of their attachment would marry them. Let them reform first. Also, avoid marrying a drunkard for the same reasons. Intemperance is a disease arising from perverted alimentiveness, and it is very difficult to cure. Don't rely on promises of abstinence; insist upon his reforming before marriage.

THE TEMPERAMENTS

Fig. 11.
The Vital Temperament.

Fig. 12.
The Mental Temperament.

We have already intimated that the Temperament is an important factor in the law of choice. It will be self-evident to those who are the least acquainted with Physiology why a predominantly Vital temperament is indicated by a broad head, thick neck and a broad-set body. The Mental temperament is indicated by a slender body, thin neck, small features, comparatively large brain, fine hair, small bones and a very susceptible mind.

Though such a union might in some respects be

beneficial to their offspring the life of the wife with the Mental temperament would be materially shortened if she were united to a man with a strong Vital temperament, while the latter would feel disappointed with his choice in consequence of there being no natural affinity between them. Neither should the Vital temperament be united to the Vital, lest there be too much impulse and sameness in the family. Variety being the spice of life, there should be such a combination as would be mutually attractive. In many respects there should be a similarity of tastes and disposition, but where there is too much of one element it would lead to discord; and wherever extremes of temperament meet, harmony and happiness cannot be expected. Persons of either sex in whom the Vital temperament predominates should be united to partners with a conspicuous Motive temperament, combined with a fair blending of the Mental and Vital parts. Such matches usually turn out well for both husband and wife as well as offspring, especially when the mental conditions are also favourable.

Those who posses but moderate Vitality and are of medium stature, as in Fig. 14, should marry partners who are nearly like themselves in these respects, especially where there is a natural affinity for each other. Such matches are suitable for husband and wife, but too numerous a progeny should be avoided, otherwise they would be likely to transmit weak and debilitated conditions of body to their children.

The highly nervous or Mental temperament

Fig. 13. a) Vital Temperament; b) Motive Temperament.

Fig. 14. Moderate Vitality.

(Fig. 12) should be blended with full Vital, well-balanced temperament (Fig. 13).

When there is a predominance of the masculine elements in one sex there should be more of the feminine in the other. Generally speaking, masculine women (Fig. 17) should marry effeminate men (Fig. 18) were it not for the fact that the former would experience a feeling of contempt for

Fig. 15.
Nervous and Dyspeptic.

Fig. 16.
Well-balanced
Temperament.

the latter, who would have the life of a toad under a harrow.

Ladies possessing strong muscular powers and positive minds are not always satisfied with attending to their home duties, but they frequently want to change places with their husbands. Large women, however, are sometimes gentle and effeminate although this is the exception rather than the rule. Some of the feminine gender become bulky, though not born to length and strength of limb and body. Very large and fleshy women are not so active, tractable, energetic and enterprising as those who are rather slight and tall; it consequently follows that if a man wishes to have a wife who is winsome, active, and a real helpmeet—one who will assist him in all that he undertakes—he should avoid marrying a woman who is very bulky and fleshy, inasmuch as it requires urgent motives to call out her physical and mental energies, and she does not usually like to be bothered very much. It is true, however, that large women have more power than small or thin ones; they may be compared to a large steamship that can carry a heavy load, but it requires some effort to get it in motion and a deal of fuel to propel it along. She also requires skilful handling, and unless there be a captain on board who is well acquainted with all her bearings, she is not likely to be a very manageable craft.

Persons in whom the Lymphatic Temperament

Fig. 17. Masculine and Positive.

Fig. 18. Deficient in Positiveness.

(Fig. 19) is very prominent should marry those in whom the Motive and Mental predominate (Fig. 20) in order that the latter may stimulate the former, and the former have a restraining influence over the latter.

Predominant Motive and Mental Temperaments (Fig. 21) should be united to those in whom the Vital powers are fairly represented (as seen in Fig. 16). If they were to be united to a partner in whom the same qualities predominate (as seen in Fig. 20), there would be too much warmth, intensity, and tenacity of feeling in the family, but in other respects the match would be favourable.

Ladies who possess thick necks, large chins, broad-set bodies and large features (Fig. 22) should never marry gentlemen whose necks, chins, chests, and features are very small (Fig. 23), otherwise there could not be a natural affinity for each other. On the other hand, a lady who has a thin neck, small chin, mouth and features in general should marry a husband who is rather tall and sprightly rather than one who has a broad head, thick neck

Fig. 19. Lymphatic Temperament.

and a robust condition of body.

If a lady has a large chin and red lips, the faculty of Amativeness will be active, even if it be not a predominant trait of her character; consequently she will have a strong desire 'to love

Fig. 20. Motive and Mental Temperament.

and be loved', to caress, kiss and fondle. If she should marry a husband in whom the chin is receding, the lips livid and white, he will care nothing for caressing and fondling. This would be unfortunate, for she would desire to receive the caresses and attentions of her husband and he would not be inclined to accord them: hence it is quite natural that she should feel slighted, ill-used and neglected. On the other hand, if the husband has a large chin and full red lips he will be loving, warm-hearted and full of affection; and if the wife has a small chin and thin white lips she will consider his attempts to caress, kiss and fondle her as obtrusive and objectionable; hence it is clear that these persons who have red lips and large

30

chins should be united to those who possess similar characteristics.

Fig. 21. Motive and Mental Temperament.

Positiveness of mind is indicated by a large nose and a stiff upper lip. Those who have these signs largely represented should marry partners in whom these traits are not so predominant, unless they each have well-trained minds; hence it is quite evident that a man who has a large and stiff upper lip should marry a woman with a smaller or loose upper lip.

If the nose of one partner is large, that of the other should be somewhat smaller. A person possessing a Roman or aquiline nose should marry one whose nose is straight, or that turns up a little.

If the nose of one´is very sharp, the nose of the

Fig. 22. Vital Temperament and Self-assurance.

other should be more blunt, because if the noses of both were equally sharp, there would be too much intensity of feeling in the family, for sharpness of nose indicates sharpness of temper.

Females whose mouths are small are not well adapted to large-featured, broad-set and robust men; hence it is much better that broad-headed or broad-built men should marry those whose mouths are well-proportioned to a well-developed physical organisation.

Those who have but little hair should marry those whose hair is more plentiful. Those who are fond of music should marry partners whose ears are beautifully rounded and stand out a little from the head. This indicates musical taste, and implies that the wife who has marked musical abilities would be most happily mated to a husband with at least a fair development of musical capacity;

Fig. 23. Small chin and neck, indicating feeble love.

otherwise he **may** consider that she is wasting time, and interfering with his occupations and pleasures, when she is practising her voice in singing and her fingers in playing the piano.

Active-minded, rapid-moving and very enterprising people (Fig. 26) should marry those who are somewhat calm and deliberate; still it is not wise for them to marry slow and tame individuals (Fig. 27), otherwise their tameness would jar upon the susceptible natures of those who are of an active turn.

Those whose heads are small in the coronal lobe (Fig. 28) should be united to those whose moral faculties are a little larger; however there should not be a very marked difference in this respect, otherwise there might be many religious contests across the breakfast table, and a considerable amount of chaffing where matters of principle are

Fig. 24.
Love, pure and platonic, rather than passionate or powerful.

Fig. 25.
Love, pure and exalted, rather than gross or carnal.

involved, to say nothing of religious differences which might exist to such an extent as to produce discord and angry feelings. There would be very little harmony between husband and wife if one were an infidel and the other a Christian, or if one were a Catholic and the other a Protestant.

Fig. 26. Activity Large.

Thus we should recommend the following as general rules:

Those who are neither very tall nor very short, whose eyes are neither very black nor very blue, whose hair is neither very black nor very red—the mixed types—may marry those who are quite similar in form, complexion and temperament to themselves.

Bright red hair and a florid complexion indicate an excitable temperament, and such should marry the jet-black hair and the brunette type.

The grey, blue, black or hazel eyes should not marry those of the same colour; where the colour is very pronounced, the union should be with those of a decidedly different colour.

Fig. 27. Tame, quiet, and unobtrusive.

The very corpulent should unite with the very thin and spare, and the short, thick-set should choose a different constitution.

The thin, bony, wiry, prominent-featured, Roman-nosed, cold-blooded individual should marry the round-featured, warm-hearted and emotional. Thus the cool should unite with warmth and suscepti-bility.

Fig. 28.	Fig. 29.
Small Veneration, and no desire to worship.	Strong moral and religious sentiments.

The extremely irritable and nervous should unite with the lymphatic, the slow and the quiet. Thus the stolid will be prompted by the nervous companion, while the excitable will be quieted by the gentleness of the less nervous.

The quick motioned, rapid-speaking person should marry the calm and deliberate; the warmly impulsive should unite with the stoical.

DIFFERENCE OF AGE

It is not wise for an old man to marry a young woman (Fig. 30) inasmuch as this is strongly opposed to nature, and the love feelings cannot be so perfectly reciprocated as when there is less disparity of age. The power of fecundity ceasing with one party is sometimes the cause of driving the other to debauchery, and the wife to jealousy;

and when offspring result from such ill-assorted unions the children are usually delicate in body and effeminate in mind. Nature avenges her outraged laws in this and other ways we need not particularise.

Fig. 30. May and December; unequally yoked.

COURTSHIP

LOVE'S TELEGRAPH—If a gentleman wants a wife, he wears a ring on the *first* finger of the left hand; if he be engaged, he wears it on the *second* finger; if married, on the *third*; and on the *fourth* if he never intends to be married. When a lady is not engaged, she wears a hoop or diamond on her *first* finger; if engaged, on the *second*; if married on the *third*; and on the *fourth* if she intends to die unmarried.

When a gentleman presents a fan, flower, or trinket to a lady with the *left* hand, this, on his part, is an overture of regard; should she receive it with the *left* hand it is considered as an acceptance of his esteem, but if with the *right* hand it is a refusal of his offer. Thus, by a few simple tokens explained by rule, the passion of love is expressed, and through the medium of the telegraph the most timid and diffident man may, without difficulty, communicate his sentiments of regard to a lady and, in case his offer be should refused, avoid the mortification of an explicit refusal.

GENERAL ETIQUETTE

On all occasions when a number of people convene together, whether indoors or out, the laws of courtesy should be obeyed. It is the duty of the gentlemen to be ever attentive to the ladies. If it be a picnic, the gentlemen will carry the luncheon, erect the swings, construct the tables, bring the water, provide the fuel for boiling the tea, etc. On the fishing excursion they will furnish the tackle, bait the hooks, row the boats, carry the fish, and furnish comfortable seats for the ladies. In gathering nuts, they will climb the trees, do the shaking, carry the nuts, and assist the ladies across the streams and over the fences. If possible, crossing the fields, go through the bars or gateway and avoid the necessity of compelling the ladies to clamber over the fences. Should it be necessary to climb them, it is etiquette for the gentleman to go over first, and when the lady is firmly on the top, he will gently help her down.

It is not etiquette for a young lady to visit a place of public amusement with a gentleman, alone, with whom she is but slightly acquainted. Her escort should the first time invite another member of the family to accompany her.

The gentleman should make a point of extending his invitation to the lady long enough before the entertainment to be able to secure desirable seats. Most of the pleasure of the occasion will depend upon being so seated as to witness the performance to advantage.

The lady having received a note of invitation, she should reply to the same immediately, that the gentleman may make his arrangements accordingly.

Should the weather be stormy, and for other reasons, it will be a very graceful way of complimenting the lady to provide a carriage for the occasion.

Any gentleman who may continuously give special undivided attention to a certain lady is presumed to do so because he prefers her to others. It is to be expected that the lady will appreciate the fact, and her feelings are likely to become engaged. Should she allow an intimacy thus to ripen upon the part of the gentleman, and to continue, it is to be expected that he will be encouraged to hope for her hand, and hence it is the duty of both lady and gentleman, if neither intends marriage, to discourage an undue intimacy which may ripen into love, as it is in the highest degree dishonourable to trifle with the affections of another. If, however, neither has any objections to the other, the courtship may continue.

THE DECLARATION OF LOVE

The young man who is desirous of gaining the love of an estimable lady should not be too bold and abrupt in making his love known to her; but he should watch his opportunity, and, if she has any brothers or friends, try to gain their esteem and good wishes, so that through them he may secure an introduction. He should not, of course, go and bluntly tell them what his business is; but if they happen to belong to a cricket club or anything of that kind, he might also become a member, and when sufficiently acquainted with them invite them to take tea with him, and, in common civility, they may return the invitation, by which means he will obtain an introduction to their sister. If this course of procedure is not convenient there would be no harm in writing a respectful letter to the lady avowing the affection inspired. When a lady receives such a letter she should not in the heat of the moment hasten to reply, but should think it over and place it under her pillow at night and sleep upon it, and next morning, when she has collected her thoughts, she may answer it. Some ladies think it derogatory to answer such communications, and they sometimes throw them into the fire immediately; but it is the duty of everyone, rich or poor, to answer a missive of this kind.

Suppose you are a young man and have made an appointment to meet a lady—do not whistle outside the gate, nor tap at the window, but walk up to the door manfully and knock. Perhaps the mother may answer the door, and if so, you scarcely know what to do or say. But a little reflection will help you out of this dilemma. You can explain that you have come on important business, and that if she will kindly allow you to enter the house you will explain your errand. On entering the house you would probably say that a few days ago you sent a letter to her daughter announcing the esteem you felt for her, and that you had come with honourable intentions and with a desire to compare notes with a view to matrimony. The mother may at first be indignant, but remember that 'faint heart never won fair lady.' Surprise is often only natural, and even stiffness or coldness may be excused. However, whilst you are speaking the daughter will not be far away, and her appearance on the scene may put all to rights eventually. If, however, the parents are unreasonably and obstinately opposed to any young man making approaches to their daughter, she will no doubt be able to contrive to be somewhere outside the house when you are expected, and thereby prevent any unpleasantness with her parents. If your offer is not accepted after comparing notes, act manfully and do not go down on your knees to beg the lady, you may bias her mind still more against you.

PARENTAL CONSENT

It is said that, in the olden times of our country, the women made the advances, and often became the suitors; but it is not upon record whether they asked the consent of their future fathers-in-law.

In many cases where the lady possesses a large fortune, or where the gentleman has little besides love to offer, it is considered the most honourable course for him to seek the parents' consent, and to ask their permission to lay his heart at her feet. Nervous, timid suitors often try to evade this trying ordeal by writing their petition instead of preferring it personally, which is but a weak mode of procedure, for should the consent be given it is only a postponement of the inevitable; and should it be witheld the chance is lost of trying persuasive eloquence, or of offering further explanations.

THE FIRST KISS

During the time of courtship it becomes rather a
knotty question as to when the young man should
venture to take the first kiss. If he be of a lively,
versatile and social nature, possessing a considerable
amount of magnetism, he will naturally attract
the young lady to him very soon. In this case, he
might be tempted to desire a kiss the first night;
but that would be rather premature. The second
night he may make rather bolder advances and
take his first kiss. We think, however, that he
would be a coward if he did not take a kiss on the
third visit. Lovers should not go further than a
chaste kiss previous to marriage, but conduct
themselves with perfect propriety, purity and
chastity. If a man's love be pure, he cannot
commit an impure act or indulge even in wicked
thought or desire towards the woman he loves.
But if a man waits too long before taking the first
kiss, his courtship is likely to be unduly protracted.
Some lovers are very bashful and slow-paced
suitors. The Reverend John Brown, of Haddington,
was one of these very bashful wooers. He courted
his lady-love for seven years; for six-and-a-half years
of this period he had got no further than on the

first six days. This state of things became intolerable, and he determined to bring the matter to a crisis. Summoning all his courage after sitting a long time, as usual, in silence, he exclaimed: 'Janet, we have been acquainted now for six years and mair, and I've never gotten a kiss yet. Do you think I might take one, my bonnie lassie?' 'Just as you like John, only be becoming and proper we' it', was the reply. 'Surely, Janet, we will ask a blessing.' The blessing was asked, the kiss taken, and the worthy divine, overpowered with the blissful sensation, most rapturously exclaimed, 'Oh, woman, but it is good! We will return thanks.' Six months after this saw the pious couple man and wife.

As a rule, ladies do not care to be asked for the first kiss; maiden modesty is a sufficient barrier to their giving consent. It naturally follows that the first kiss should be taken without being asked for; a scuffle sufficient to lend the affair excitement is almost sure to follow, but this only lends enchantment to it, and it will be more highly appreciated by both genders.

POPPING THE QUESTION

Some young lovers are very diffident and find it difficult to screw up their courage to 'pop the question', lest they should 'put their foot in it.' Undoubtedly, making a declaration of love is one of the most trying ordeals to which a man can be subjected, requiring more resolution than facing the cannon's mouth. We should like to help the bashful young man to come creditably through this ordeal; but it is impossible to give any specific directions how to proceed in every case. The great thing is to screw up your courage to the speaking point. If you cannot do this, you may put your request in writing. But whether you write or speak, let your enquiry be clearly understood.

When a man whose love is deep and sincere ventures to 'pop the question', he may evince a considerable amount of diffidence and awkwardness, and may even make himself appear very foolish in many ways, but this is a sure sign that he is under the powerful influence of love; hence the lady may safely answer in the affirmative. Those, on the other hand, who pay polite attentions, flatter the young ladies, and make personal remarks, even of an eulogistic nature, or stare them straight in the eyes, with their own wide open, and 'pop the question' in a cool and composed manner, and without confusion, are not so deep in love as to be fully depended on, inasmuch as theirs is a species of admiration rather than of pure love. When a lady feels that she loves the man who has proposed to her sufficient to marry him, her answer should be from the heart and not of an evasive nature. Some girls say 'No' when they mean 'Yes', and many have lived to repent. Very few men who are worth having care to propose a second time, lest they should have the mortification of a second refusal. Some ladies, however, find it difficult to answer the question, and feel as though they cannot utter a word; when this is the case you may publish the banns at once, for 'silence gives consent'. A gentleman who was once very diffident, and felt desirous of 'popping the question', scarcely knew how to do it; but after a little consideration he felt that he had sufficient courage to ask the pet canary, to which he said, 'Dicky, may I marry your mistress?' It was answered by the lady, who said, 'Say yes, my birdie.'

For those who find a similar difficulty in introducing the subject, here are some suggestions as to how a gentleman may overcome this predicament. He may write to the lady, making an offer, and request her to reply. He may, if he dare not trust to words, even in her presence write the question on a slip of paper, and request her laughingly to give a plain 'no' or 'yes.' He may ask her if in case a gentleman very much like himself was to make a proposal of marriage to her, what would she say. She will probably laughingly reply that it will be time enough to tell what she would say when the proposal is made. He may jokingly remark that he intends one of these days to ask a certain lady not a thousand miles away if she will marry him, and asks what her answer she supposes the lady will give him; she will quite likely reply that it will depend upon what lady he asks. And thus he may approach the subject, by agreeable and easy stages, in a hundred ways, depending upon the circumstances.

BETROTHAL, OR ENGAGEMENT

In Holland all the friends and neighbours of the engaged couple assemble and celebrate the betrothal by an extensive consumption of *bruidssuiker*—bridal sugar, and *bruidstranen*—bridal tears, as the spiced wine drunk on that occasion is called. In England it was once the custom to break in half a gold or silver coin, in token of a verbal contract and a promise of love, but now it is the fashion for the fiancé to give his fiancée a ring of a plain though handsome description. Superstition forbids the ring being set with either opals or emeralds—the former because they denote change, the latter jealousy.

CONDUCT DURING THE ENGAGEMENT

The engaged couple should not appear in public without a chaperon—an office which, though an honorary one, is generally deemed to be a laborious post, and on occasions even a disagreeable one. For it cannot be agreeable to be in the position of being one too many, and where you are not wanted. This third person who plays propriety is also known by the name of 'Gooseberry.'

The gentleman should be upon pleasant terms with the lady's family, making himself agreeable to her parents, her sisters and her brothers. Especially to the younger members of her family should the gentleman render his presence agreeable, by occasional rides and little favours, presents of sweetmeats, etc. He should also take pains to comply with the general regulations of the family during his visits, being punctual at meals and early in retiring, kind and courteous to servants, and agreeable to all. He should still be gallant to the ladies, but never so officiously attentive to anyone as to arouse uneasiness upon the part of his affianced. Neither should he expect her to eschew the society of gentlemen entirely from the time of her engagement.

The lady he has chosen for his future companion is supposed to have good sense, and while she may be courteous to all, receiving visits and calls, she will allow no flirtations, nor do anything calculated to excite jealousy on the part of her fiancé.

Visits should not be unduly protracted. If the gentleman makes them in the evening they should be made early and should not be over two hours in length. The custom of remaining until a late hour has passed away in genteel society. Such conduct at the present time, among the acquaintance of the lady, is certain to endanger her reputation.

The lovers should not be so entirely absorbed with each other as to ignore or neglect others whose company they may be in, nor is it considered good manners to display demonstrative affection continually, or publicly. 'All frothy tendernesses and amorous boilings-over are insults on, and affronts to company', says Swift.

Should a misunderstanding or quarrel happen, it should be removed by the lady making the first advances towards a reconciliation. She thus shows a magnanimity which can but win admiration from her lover. Let both in their conduct towards each other be confiding, noble and generous.

As a rule, long courtships are undesirable. Courtship is the time for comparing notes with each other in regard to tastes, qualities, adaptation, position in life, education, etc., each of which can be ascertained in a few months as well as in as many years. If long courtships are indulged in the parties are wasting some of their most precious time. The proper period for basking in the sunshine of each other's love is after, rather than before, marriage. In long courtships, unpleasant questions may crop up. Some time ago, we met with a gentleman who had been courting a young lady for about eight years. At length they were to be married, and on their way to Church the bridegroom asked his affianced if she would be willing to clean his boots when they were married. She indignantly answered 'No, I will not.' 'Well then,' he said, 'I am off back again.' This question should not have been asked before marriage.

MARRIAGE

Some of the popular expressions about marriage imply a belief that it is like a game of chance or a lottery, with one prize to a thousand blanks. That is a cynical view of marriage, like the rather profane saying that if matches are made in heaven, they are dipped in the other place! Those who are unequally yoked will believe this adage to be true, but those between whom there is a harmony of physical and mental conditions will consider marriage to be a heaven upon earth; but this can only be attained by a proper adaptation of husband to wife.

An imperative duty which married people owe to each other is fidelity to the marriage vow. This is a duty so sacred that the least suspicion cast on it will throw a blight over their happiness. By fidelity we mean not only the avoidance of gross and open outrage of the conjugal covenant, but flirtations and all acts which give any occasion for jealousy. Beware of trifling with the vows you made at the altar, and let each join in chorus and say:—

Fig. 31. Badly mated.

Through shade and sunshine, ever still the same,
Dreaming of thee:
I would not, could not, change, whate'er betide,
But constant be.

To cultivate a cheerful disposition is another desirable feature of married life. All persons are not equally endowed with a hopeful spirit, but the model husband and wife should cultivate cheerfulness. Husbands and wives should take pleasant walks, rural excursions and rambles together in the fields, during which they should hold frequent conversations on subjects of interest and importance to them both.

Fig. 32. Too much sameness in the Family.

ETIQUETTE OF MARRIAGE

Banns must be published *three* times in the parish church, in *each place* where the persons concerned reside. The clerk is applied to on such occasions. When the marriage ceremony is over, the parties repair to the vestry and enter their names in the parish registry. The registry is signed by the clergyman and the witnesses present, and a certificate of the registry is given to the bridegroom. The charge for a certificate of marriage is standard, but the clergyman's fee varies according to the circumstances. The clerk will at all times give information thereupon; and it is best for a friend of the bridegroom to attend to the pecuniary arrangements.

WEDDING DRESS

It is impossible to lay down specific rules for dress, as fashions change, and tastes differ. History tells us that the dress of one royal lady was composed of velvet and cloth of gold, and the weight of it was sixty pounds! Brides of the present day are dressed entirely in white, unless for a second marriage, when it is usual to choose some delicate colour, such as silver-grey or dove-colour, and also to wear a bonnet instead of the virgin veil. The wearing of the veil appears to have originated with the Anglo-Saxons, whose custom it was to perform the ceremony under a square piece of cloth which was held at each corner by a tall man over the bridegroom and the bride, for the purpose of concealing her blushes. A wreath of white flowers is worn under the veil, white gloves and boots, and a bouquet composed entirely of white flowers. Any great display of jewellery is in bad taste, and the little that may be allowed should not be of a florid or elaborate kind. The dress of Richard Coeur de Lion as a bridegroom was a satin tunic of a rose colour, belted round the waist; a mantle of striped silver tissue, brocaded with silver crescents; and on his head a rose-coloured bonnet, brocaded in gold with figures of animals. The bridegroom of today is dressed in morning attire—dark blue frock-coat, white waistcoat, trousers of some very light shade, and a scarf or tie of a delicate tint. But the great art consists in selecting the style of dress most becoming to the person. A stout person should adopt a different style from a thin person; a tall one from a short one. Peculiarities of complexion and form of face and figure should be duly regarded; and in these matters there is no better course than to call in the aid of any respectable milliner and dressmaker, who will be found ready to give the best advice. The bridegroom should simply appear in full dress, and should avoid everything eccentric and broad in style. The bridesmaids should always be made aware of the bride's dress before they choose their own, which should be determined by a proper harmony with the former.

THE WEDDING

The bridegroom should send a carriage at his expense for the officiating clergyman and his family. He is not expected to pay for the carriage of the parents of the bride, nor for those occupied by the bridesmaids and groomsmen. The latter will furnish the carriages for the ladies, unless otherwise provided. The invited guests will go in carriages at their own expense.

THE ORDER OF GOING TO CHURCH

The BRIDE, accompanied by her *father*, not infrequently her *mother*, and uniformly by a *bridesmaid*, occupies the *first carriage*. The father hands out the bride, and leads her to the altar, the mother and the bridesmaid following. After them come the other bridesmaids, attended by the groomsmen, if there are more than one.

The BRIDEGROOM occupies the *last carriage* with the principal *groomsman*—an intimate friend or brother. He follows, and stands facing the altar, with *the bride at his left hand*. The father places himself behind, with the mother, if she attends.

The *chief bridesmaid* occupies a place on the *left* of the *bride*, to hold her gloves and handkerchief and flowers; her *companions* range themselves on the *left*. If any difficulties arise from forgetfulness, the vestrywoman can set everything right.

THE CEREMONY

In some churches both bride and groom remove the right-hand glove. When a ring is used, it is the duty of the first bridesmaid to remove the bride's left-hand glove. An awkward pause is, however, avoided by opening one seam of the glove upon the ring finger, and at the proper time the glove may be turned back, and the ring thus easily placed where it belongs, which is the third finger of the left hand.

The responses of the bride and groom should not be too hastily nor too loudly given.

REMEMBER TO TAKE THE LICENCE AND THE RING WITH YOU.

WEDDING RINGS

The custom of wearing wedding rings appears to have taken its rise among the Romans. Before the celebration of their nuptials there was a meeting of friends at the house of the lady's father, to settle articles of the marriage contract, when it was agreed that the dowry should be paid down on the wedding day or soon after. On this occasion there was commonly a feast, at the conclusion of which the man gave to the woman, as a pledge, a ring, which she put on the third finger of her left hand, *because it was believed that an artery reached thence to the heart*, and a day was then named for the wedding.

WHY THE WEDDING RING IS PLACED ON THE THIRD FINGER

'We have remarked on the vulgar error which supposes that an artery runs from the third finger of the left hand to the heart. It is said by Swinburn and others that therefore it became the wedding finger. The priesthood kept up this idea by still retaining it as the wedding finger, but the custom is really associated with the doctrine of the Trinity: for, in the ancient ritual of English marriages, the ring was placed by the husband on the top of the left hand, with the words "In the name of the Father"; he then removed it to the forefinger, saying, "In the name of the Son"; then to the second finger, adding, "And of the Holy Ghost"; finally, he left it as now, on the third finger, with the closing word "Amen".' . . . *The History of Poetry and Finger Rings.*

WHEN THE CEREMONY IS CONCLUDED

The bride, taking the bridegroom's arm, goes into the vestry, the others following; signatures are then affixed, and a registration made, after which the married pair enter their carriage and proceed to the breakfast, everyone else following.

Our newly-wedded grandmothers were heartily kissed as soon as the service was concluded, by their husbands and relatives, new and old. Our mothers were more prudish, and waited for the seclusion of the vestry before offering their fair cheeks. Our grandfathers were adorned with huge rosettes which they called 'true-love knots', made of various coloured ribbons; these they wore on their hats, both on their nuptial day and for several weeks after. Our fathers wore smaller ones of white pinned on the breast of their coats, which they called 'favours.' Their sons do not exhibit these decorations, which only appear on servants in these days.

Only the bridegroom is congratulated at the wedding; it is he who is supposed to have won the prize.

differs only from the going in the fact that the bride and bridegroom now ride together, the bride being on his left, and a bridesmaid and a groomsman, or the father of the bride, occupying the front seats of the carriage.

THE WEDDING BREAKFAST

The wedding breakfast having already been prepared, the wedding party return thereto. If a large party, the bride and bridegroom occupy seats in the centre of the long table, and the two extremities should be presided over by elderly relatives, if possible one from each family. Everybody should endeavour to make the occasion as happy as possible. One of the senior members of either the bride or bridegroom's family should, some time before the breakfast has terminated, rise, and in a brief but graceful manner propose the 'Health and happiness of the wedded pair.' It is much better to drink their healths together than separately; and, after a brief interval, the bridegroom should return thanks, which he may do without hesitation, since no one looks for a speech upon such an occasion. A few words, feelingly expressed, are all that is required. Wedding cake and wine are handed round, of which everyone partakes, and each expresses some kindly wish for the newly married pair. The breakfast generally concludes with the departure of the happy pair upon their wedding tour.

WEDDING CAKES

Four pounds of fine flour, well dried; four pounds of fresh butter; two pounds of loaf sugar; a quarter of a pound of mace, pounded and sifted fine; the same of nutmegs. To every pound of flour, add eight eggs; wash four pounds of currants, let them be well-picked and dried before the fire; blanch a pound of sweet almonds, and cut them lengthwise very thin; a pound of citron; one pound of candied orange; the same of candied lemon; half a pint of brandy. When these are made ready, work the butter with your hand to a cream, then beat in the sugar a quarter-of-an-hour; beat the whites of the eggs to a very strong froth; mix them with the sugar and butter; beat the yolks half an hour at least, and mix them with the cake; then put in the flour, mace, and nutmeg, and keep beating well till your oven is ready; pour in the brandy, and beat the currants and almonds lightly in. Tie three sheets of white paper round the bottom of your hoop to keep it from running out; rub it well with butter; put in your cake; lay the sweetmeats in layers, with cake between each layer, and after it is risen and coloured, cover it up with paper before your oven is stopped up. It will require three hours to bake properly.

ALMOND ICING FOR WEDDING CAKES

Beat the whites of three eggs to a strong froth; pulp a pound of Jordan almonds very fine with rose water; mix them, with the eggs, lightly together; put in by degrees a pound of common loaf sugar in powder. When the cake is baked enough, take it out, and lay on the icing; then put it in to brown.

SUGAR ICING FOR WEDDING CAKES

Beat two pounds of double refined sugar with two ounces of fine starch, sift the whole through a gauze sieve, then beat the whites of five eggs with a knife upon a pewter dish for half an hour; beat in the sugar a little at a time, or it will make the eggs fall and injure the colour. When all the sugar is put in, beat it half an hour longer, and then lay on your almond icing, spreading it even with a knife. If put on as soon as the cake comes out of the oven, it will harden by the time the cake is cold.

THE WEDDING TOUR

Upon departure on the wedding tour, the bride's travelling dress should be very quiet and modest, and not such as in any way to attract attention.

The custom of throwing old shoes is long established, and one which royalty does not disdain to use at the present day. It is said to have been a symbol of renunciation, on the part of the bride's father, of all authority and dominion over her. Now it is merely regarded as wishing good luck—a piece of nonsense useful for distracting and turning the thoughts, and making merriment at a somewhat trying moment. Those guests who are not strictly speaking part of the wedding party should take their leave directly after the departure of the happy couple; it is rather a tax upon the hosts to provide amusements and keep up the spirits of the party throughout this long, long day. The wisest thing to do is to send all the young people for a drive—croquet is rather too fatiguing a pastime after such a morning's work.

The wedding tour must depend upon the tastes and circumstances of the married couple. Home-loving Englishmen and women may find much to admire and enjoy without ranging abroad. Those whose time is somewhat restricted we recommend to sojourn at Tunbridge Wells—Mount Ephraim is especially to be selected—and thence the most delightful excursions may be made to different parts of the country. Those who like sketching, botanising, and collecting seaweeds will find ample opportunities for these; those who like old ruins and time-hallowed places may reach them without difficulty: Dover, Canterbury, Folkestone and Tatwood Castle are all within reach; and what places are more deeply interesting, not only in respect of scenery, but historic associations? Cornwall and Devonshire, the Isle of Wight, &c., are each delightful to the tourist; and the former is now accessible by railway almost as far as Land's End. The scenery of the north of Devon, and of both coasts of Cornwall, is especially beautiful. North Wales offers a delightful excursion; the lakes of Westmorland and Cumberland; the lakes of Killarney, in Ireland; also the magnificent scenery of the Scottish lakes and mountains. To those who wish for a wider range, France, Germany, Switzerland, and the Rhine offer charms which cannot be surpassed.

CARDS

A newly married pair send out cards immediately after the ceremony to their friends and acquaintances who, on their part, return either notes or cards of congratulation on the event. As soon as the lady is settled in her new home, she may expect the calls of her acquaintances; for which it is not absolutely necessary to remain at home, although politeness requires that any calls should be returned as soon as possible. But, having performed this, any further intercourse may be avoided (where it is deemed necessary) by a polite refusal of invitations. Where cards are to be left, the number must be determined according to the various members of which the family called upon is composed. For instance, where there are the mother, aunt and daughters (the latter having been introduced to society) three cards should be left. Recently, the custom of sending cards has been in a great measure discontinued, and instead of this the words 'No cards' are appended to the ordinary announcement of the marriage, and the announcement of the marriage, with this addition, is considered all sufficient.

The bride ought not to receive visitors without a mother, or sister, or some friend being present—not even if her husband be at home. Gentlemen who are in professions, or have Government appointments, cannot always await the arrival of visitors; when such is the case, some old friend of the family should represent the husband, and proffer an apology for his absence.

MARRIAGE BY REGISTRATION

An act was passed in the reign of William the Fourth, by which it was rendered legal for persons wishing to be married by a civil ceremony to give notice of their intention to the Registrar of Marriages in their district or districts. Three weeks' notice is necessary, to give which the parties call, separately or together, at the office of the registrar, who enters their names in a book. When the time of notice has expired, it is only necessary to give the registrar an intimation on the previous day of your intention to attend at his office on the next day, and complete the registration. The ceremony consists of merely answering a few questions, and making the declaration that you take each other to live as husband and wife. The fee amounts to only a few shillings, and in this form no wedding ring is required, though it is usually placed on in the presence of the persons assembled. The married couple receive a certificate of marriage, which is in every respect lawful.

FOREIGN WEDDINGS

In France the law is very strict on the question of time, and severe indeed is the punishment if its bounds are overstepped: 'The rite of marriage is to be performed between the hours of eight a.m. and twelve, upon pain of suspension and felony with fourteen years' transportation.'

There is an Eastern country wherein the custom is for the bride, after the marriage ceremony—which is performed in the forenoon—to sit for the remainder of the day in complete silence in a corner of the room, with her face to the wall. This silence, it appears, is intended to typify the sorrow of the bride at changing her condition.

CURIOSITIES OF MARRIAGE

Goethe said that he married to obtain respectability, and Wycherly, in his old age, married his servant girl to spite his relations. The giving of a ring is supposed to indicate the eternity of the union, seeing that a circle is endless. Among the Jews the rule was for a maiden to marry on the fourth and a widow on the fifth day of the week—not earlier—and the bride is set on the right in the ceremony, while throughout Christendom her place is on the left. In a Roman marriage the bride was purchased by the bridegroom's payment of three pieces of copper money to her parents. The custom of putting a veil upon the maid before the betrothal was done to conceal her blushes at the first touch of the man's hand and at the closing kiss. Kissing the bride the moment the marriage ceremony ended, though not now prescribed, was formerly an imperative act on the part of the bridegroom. The early marriage ceremony among the Anglo-Saxons consisted merely of hand-fastening, or taking each other by the hand, and pledging each other love and affection in the presence of friends and relatives. An old adage lays down the proper days for wedlock thus:—

'Monday for wealth, Tuesday for health,
Wednesday the best day of all;
Thursday for crosses, Friday for losses,
Saturday no luck at all.'

Polyandry, or *Polyandria*: that form of polygamy which permits a woman to have several husbands. The hot-bed of Polyandry is Tibet.

ADVICE TO HUSBANDS

You can hardly imagine how refreshing it is to occasionally call up the recollection of your courting days. How tediously the hours rolled away prior to the appointed time of meeting; how swiftly they seemed to fly when you had met; how fond was the first greeting; how tender the last embrace; how fervent were your vows; how vivid your dreams of future happiness, when, returning to your home, you felt yourself secure in the confessed love of the object of your warm affections! Is your dream realised? Are you as happy as you expected? Consider whether, as a husband, you are as fervent and constant as you were when a lover. Remember that the wife's claims to your unremitting regard, great before marriage, are now exalted to a much higher degree. She has left the world for you—the home of her childhood, the fireside of her parents; their watchful care and sweet intercourse have all been yielded up for you. Look, then, most jealously upon all that may tend to attract you from home and weaken that union upon which your temporal happiness mainly depends; and believe that in the solemn relationship between husband and wife is to be found one of the best guarantees for man's honour and happiness.

If your wife complains that young ladies 'now-a-days' are very forward, do not accuse her of jealousy. A little concern on her part only proves her love for you, and you may enjoy your triumph without saying a word. Do not evince your weakness either, by complaining of every trifling neglect. What though her chair is not set so close to yours as it used to be, or though her knitting or crochet seem to absorb too large a share of her attention; depend upon it that, as her eyes watch the intertwinings of the threads and the manoeuvres of the needles as they dance in compliance to her delicate fingers, she is thinking of courting days, love-letters, smiles, tears, suspicions and reconciliations, by which your two hearts became entwined together in the net-work of love, whose meshes you can neither of you unravel or escape.

Husbands should be as attentive to their wives as they were before they were married. Do not annoy your wife by smoking in the house, or doing anything that will be a source of annoyance to her. If you have been in the habit of handing her over the stiles before marriage, do not leave her to tumble over them by herself after wedlock.

We recommend every husband to implant a loving kiss upon his wife's lips each night on returning from his daily occupation, and every morning before he goes to his business, and supplement these as often as he thinks fit. Some men, however, never think of kissing their wives from one year's end to another. When such is the case, there must be a screw loose somewhere, because wherever there is love, it will find a way of manifesting itself. As a rule, the more kisses married people give to each other the more they want. The more the flame of love is fed the brighter and more intense it becomes.

We believe that much bad temper is caused by violations of the laws of health in respect to the quality and quantity of food eaten. When people are suffering from indigestion and biliousness they cannot help feeling irritable and fault-finding. If married people would live on plain food, and be content with two meals per day, they would be much more likely to retain their balance of temper and beauty of disposition. Those who drink strong tea and coffee and eat highly-seasoned, greasy and stimulating food become irritable, nervous and desponding.

ADVICE TO WIVES

The biblical definition of a wife is a 'helpmeet', and a most expressive word it is. King Solomon, who must have been a good judge of women, said, 'Whoso findeth a wife findeth a good thing', and there can be no reasonable doubt that he used the word 'wife' in the sense of a 'helpmeet.' The etymological definition of the word 'wife' is also significant of what a true wife was in the olden times, for the word 'wife' means a weaver. It was customary in those days for the wife to weave the clothing, bed linen, etc., used in her household; and it may also be interesting to know that the unmarried women got the name of 'spinsters' because they spun the wool into the yarn which was woven by the good housewife.

Perchance you think that your husband's disposition is much changed, that he is no longer the sweet-tempered, ardent lover he used to be. But consider his struggles with the world, his everlasting race with the busy competition of trade. What is it makes him so eager in the pursuit of gain—so energetic by day, so sleepless by night—but his love of home, wife and children, and a dread that their respectability may be in peril?

If your husband occasionally looks a little troubled when he comes home, do not say to him, with an alarmed countenance, 'What ails you, my dear?' Do not bother him; he will tell you of his own accord, if need be. Do not rattle a hailstorm of fun about his ears either; be observant and quiet. Do not suppose that you are of course the cause. Let him alone until he is inclined to talk; take up your book or your needlework (pleasantly, cheerfully; no pouting, no sullenness) and wait until he is inclined to be sociable. Do not let him ever find a shirt-button missing. A shirt-button being off a collar or wristband has frequently produced the first hurricane in married life. Men's shirt-collars never fit exactly—see that your husband's are made as well as possible, and then, if he does fret a little about them, never mind it; men have a prescriptive right to fret about shirt-collars.

Never complain that your husband pores too much over the newspaper, to the exclusion of that pleasing converse which you formerly enjoyed with him. Do not hide the paper; do not give it to the children to tear; do not be sulky when the boy leaves it at the door, but take it pleasantly, and lay it down before your spouse. Think what man would be without a newspaper; treat it as a great agent in the work of civilisation—which it assuredly is; and think how much good newspapers have done by exposing bad husbands and bad wives, by giving their errors to the eye of the public. But manage you in this way: when your husband is absent, instead of gossiping with the neighbours or looking into shop windows, sit down quietly and look over that paper; run your eye over its home and foreign news; glance rapidly at the accidents and casualities; carefully scan the leading articles; and at tea-time, when your husband again takes up his paper, say, 'My dear, what an awful state of things there seems to be in India!' or, 'What a terrible calamity at Santiago!' or, 'Trade appears to be flourishing in the north'; and depend upon it, down will go the paper. If he has not read the information he will hear it all from your lips and, when you have done, he will ask, 'Did you, my dear, read Banting's letter on Corpulence?' And, whether you did or not, you will gradually get into as cosy a chat as you ever enjoyed, and you will discover that, rightly used, the newspaper is the wife's real friend, for it keeps the husband at home and supplies capital topics for every-day table-talk.

Do not *rake* up strife, otherwise you cannot have peace at home. *Plant* a smile of good temper in your face, and let your partner see your countenance suffused with the sunshine of love. *Protect* the young and tender *branches* of your family; look well after their health, and do not give them indigestible food to eat, nor unnatural drinks, otherwise they will not rise up and call you blessed. *Propagate* the tendrills of affection wherever they appear, and carefully *root out* all angry feelings, and then a good *crop* of happiness may be expected —more especially if you add to these the prompt repair of stockings, etc. It is very irritating for a husband's stockings to be out of repair to such an extent that his toes come through them. Keep the house clean and tidy, and let everything be done at its proper season. Do not let your husband wait half-an-hour for his dinner when he has to return to his business within the hour. Keep yourself neater and tidier than you did before you were married. If you had to appear respectable in order to catch your husband, you must be more particular in your dress and appearance in order to retain his love. Your dress may be made of calico, but it should be neat.

Avoid reading sensational and trashy novels, for they create impure desires and sully the feelings; and be always careful of your conduct and language; a husband is largely restrained by the chastity, purity and refinement of his wife. A lowering of dignity, a looseness of expression and vulgarity of words, may greatly lower the standard of the husband's purity of speech and morals.

Try to be as pleasant and engaging as possible to keep your husband at home. Do not listen to tale-bearing neighbours, nor believe your husband to be at fault until you have proved it, and do not make matters worse by any cutting, seething and unkind expressions, otherwise you may stifle his love and cause him to seek solace at the public-house.

ETIQUETTE FOR HUSBANDS AND WIVES

Let the rebuke be preceded by a kiss.

Do not require a request to be repeated.

Never should both be angry at the same time.

Never neglect the other, for all the world beside.

Let the angry word be answered only with a kiss.

Bestow your warmest sympathies in each other's trials.

Never make a remark calculated to bring ridicule upon the other.

Make your criticism in the most loving manner possible.

Make no display of the sacrifices you make for each other.

Never reproach the other for an error which was done with a good motive and with the best judgment at the time.

Always leave home with a tender good-bye and loving words. They may be the last.

DIVORCES IN DIFFERENT COUNTRIES

In Australia divorces have but recently been sanctioned, and they are scarcely ever known to occur in modern Greece. In Hindostan either party for a slight cause may leave the other and re-marry, but in Tibet divorces are rarely allowed, unless with the consent of both parties, and re-marriage is forbidden. In olden times the Jews had a discretionary power of divorcing their wives, whereas in Cochin China the parties desiring a divorce break a pair of chopsticks in the presence of witnesses and the thing is done. If the wife of a Turkoman asks his permission to go out, and he says 'Go', without adding 'Come back again', they are divorced. In Siberia, if a man is dissatisfied with the most trifling acts of his wife, he tears the cap or veil from her face, and that constitutes a divorce. In Siam the first wife may be divorced, but not sold as the others may be, and she may claim the first child; the others belong to the husband. Among the Moors a wife may be divorced if she does not become the mother of a boy. In the arctic regions a man who wants a divorce leaves home in anger and does not return for several days; the wife takes the hint and departs. In China divorces are allowed in all cases of criminality, mutual dislike, jealousy, incompatibility of temperament, or too much loquacity on the part of the wife. Among the Tartars, if the wife is ill-treated she complains to the magistrate, who, attended by the principal people, accompanies her to the house and pronounces a divorce.

We trust that all who read this book will never have to have recourse to the laws of divorce in greater detail than the above curious paragraph.